Poems of

Love, Life and Loss

By

Harriet Blackbury

HBlackbury

LIVE WIRE BOOKS

First published in October 2005 by
Live Wire Books
The Orchard
School Lane
Warmington
Banbury
OX17 1DE

Tel: 01295 690624
www.livewirebooks.com
info@livewirebooks.com

ISBN no. 0-9542860-7-3

Cover design by Zoe Russon
Illustrations by Chris Cable

Printed and bound in Great Britain by Antony Rowe Limited.

There is a word, a 'name of fear' which arouses terror in the heart of the vast educated majority of the English-speaking race. The most valiant will fly at the mere utterance of that word. The most broad-minded will put their backs up against it. The most rash will not dare to affront it. I myself have seen it empty buildings that had been full; and I know that it will scatter a crowd more quickly than a hose-pipe, hornets or the rumour of plague. Even to murmur it is to incur solitude, probably disdain and possibly starvation, as historical examples show.
That word is 'poetry'.

Arnold Bennett. 1867-1931

The thoughts and attitudes expressed in Harriet Blackbury's delightful texts are entirely in accordance with each title. They are sincere, touching and valuable contributions to remedying the materialism of modern lifestyles.

The late Philip W. Holland

A huge thanks to Jill, without whose true professionalism, patience and assistance this book would not have been possible.

My grateful thanks to Zoe for an inspirational cover and to Chris for bringing the book to life.

Harriet Blackbury. 2005

Contents

PILL TIME

I take eight tablets, if I remember.
Every single day.
I spread them on the worktop,
In a colourful array.

I take a water tablet
To flush my kidneys out.
Then I take a bigger white pill
To ease the pain I get with gout.

The next one contains rat poison,
I tell you not a lie,
But this, they say, is essential.
Without it I would die.

Now make some sense of that
And make the answer quick.
In case I get St. Vitas Dance
And my legs start to kick.

Next I take a capsule,
That's a lovely browny red.
I think it helps my arthritis,
Or the pain that's in my head.

Into a glass of water
An aspirin next I drop.
Sometimes I put the wrong one in
And watch it float on top.

That's when, in total confusion
I have to walk away.
I put them in the cupboard
And hope I last the day.

I save two pills for after
I've had my piece of toast.
But my husband sometimes takes them
So him, I have to roast.

I'm not sure how they affect him.
But a change is as good as a rest.
I've hidden his Viagra
As I think it's for the best.

≈

THE CHAIR TESTER

When it comes to chairs, he's sat in them all,
Even the one in the corner, against the wall.

He doesn't like the one nearest to the telly,
It gives him cramp and his foot turns to jelly.

The one in the window really cricks his neck
And when he stands up he shouts: 'Oh Heck'

Even on the sofa he has some moans,
As it wasn't made for his tired old bones.

He's tried the rocker, by the back door.
But he fell asleep and slid onto the floor!

The old recliner has safety wings,
But this plays havoc with his private 'things'.

The dining chair he finds too erect,
One hasn't been made that he finds quite perfect.

Every time he sits down to read the paper,
He springs up again, just two minutes later.

This chair tester baffles his wife, it's true,
That's why she's bought a tube of super glue.

SHE WAS WONDERFUL

She was wonderful in the garden,
All the plants she could cultivate.
She was wonderful in the kitchen,
All her dinners were just first rate.

She was wonderful in the household,
All the brass, it shone to a treat.
She was wonderful with the children,
Who made our life complete.

She was wonderful too, towards me.
Our love, it was just so deep.
But when we got to the bedroom,
Alas, she just went to sleep.

GOOD ADVICE

She gave me the soundest advice,
That has stayed with me to this day.
It was: "Save some money so when clouds appear,
You can smile till the rain clears away."

BLAST FROM THE PAST

She suddenly saw him across the room.
The man with whom she'd once had a steamy affair.
She remembered how he'd tied her to the bed,
As she abandoned every care.

Now wasn't the moment to approach him,
They were both in another space and time.
But their eyes locked in total memory,
Recalling what was then quite sublime.

Her whole body seemed to tingle,
And her head, it felt quite light.
A bright flush of redness came to her cheeks,
As she thought of that wonderful night.

A few minutes later he walked to the door.
It was impossible for either to speak.
He turned back to look at her one last time,
And suddenly her knees went quite weak.

Thank goodness that moment was over.
Thank goodness that the sun once shone.
It is all part of life's rich tapestry.
But she couldn't help wonder where he'd gone!

❧

THE MAKEOVER

I think you should have a 'makeover' dear,
To get rid of those hairs up your nose.
We'll book you in at the chiropodists too,
So she can smarten up your toes.

We'll ask the barber to de-fuzz your ears
And shave the hairs from your neck.
And give you a 'hot towel' facial.
I can hear you saying, 'Oh heck!'

We'll get your eyebrows trimmed so neat
Because they are growing quite wild.
You might need a touch of collagen too,
And a shot of botox, ever so mild.

We'll have you looking so presentable
That you'll wonder where the years have gone.
You might as well spend some money on yourself,
Now you are eighty one.

❧

SURVIVAL

She had a tough streak called survival
But it was really only a veneer.
Inside her heart was aching
And she couldn't let anyone near.

HAPPY AUGUST

I just can't seem to get on today,
I just can't get ahead.
I'm still sorting yesterday's queries
And promising leads that now seem dead.

I just can't raise my energy level.
My morale, it's very low.
Where's that boost of adrenaline gone?
I had it last week, I know.

Our monthly figures are way out,
There must be a hidden agenda!
My secretary's gone on her holiday
And left me a 'temp' called Brenda.

She doesn't know how I operate
And she makes really lousy tea.
And she has an annoying giggle,
That is definitely getting to me.

The children are driving my wife mad,
They are on their school holiday.
On top of which my in-laws have come
And are here for a fortnight's stay!

I think that I'm losing my marbles.
Roll on autumn for goodness sake.
When we can all get back to normality
After the long summer break.

SECOND CHANCE

Just when I thought I was moving on,
I felt you near to my bed.
I quickly looked up and saw nothing at all,
I thought I was going out of my head.

That night I went out and had my first date
With a guy who I'd met in the shop.
He'd lost his partner, just like me
So emotions we started to swap.

I came home thinking, 'What was the point'
Of bothering to even go out.
I felt so guilty, it was all too soon.
He was as depressed as me, without doubt.

Weeks went by and he hadn't phoned,
Which did me some good in a way.
As I'd made up my mind to say 'No thanks'
Had he rung me the very next day.

Then out of the blue I got a call
Which started to make my heart flutter.
He was in a bad way and needed a chat
He said, with a bit of a stutter.

So I went and I listened with a sympathetic ear.
The state of his mind wasn't good.
But I came home thinking how nice he was
And told him to ring whenever he could.

Well that was the start and we slowly progressed
And climbed out of the pit we were in.
We both had baggage and heartache untold
And nerves that were paper thin.

Now we are married and doing okay
And supporting each other day by day.
It hasn't been easy, sometimes two steps back
Just as one step was going our way.

But we're keeping focused and positive together
And come rain or shine, we'll get through.
Life has to go on, we have no choice
Though I still often think about you.

❧

X RAY

Xray my soul,
Love me inside out.
Take me now
So I scream out.

Love me for
The time is right.
I cannot wait
Until tonight.

Touch the passion
I feel within.
This is surely
Not a sin.

MISTAKES

Mistakes can happen when we're feeling deadbeat
And we've spent all day long just stood on our feet.

Mistakes can happen when our mind goes blank
Because of the wine that we earlier drank!

Mistakes can happen which really aren't our fault,
Like when trees jump out and give our car a jolt.

Mistakes can happen in the very strangest way
That can make us regret getting out of bed that day.

Mistakes can happen which make our blood pressure rise,
Especially when we take the blame for other people's lies.

Mistakes can happen that leave us feeling blue
But with a little humour we'll surely get through.

Mistakes can happen when our mind strays from the plot
As we recall our first love, my goodness, she was hot!

᠀

TAKE EACH DAY AS IT COMES

Let time take care of tomorrow
And you know, in the long term, it will.
Don't worry yourself with unnecessary doubts,
Life, in the end, will climb it's own hill.

HYPOCHONDRIAC

My feet are swollen, I'm having a heart attack
And I've got a pain in the middle of my back.

My blood pressure is high and my pulse is racing,
I wonder what kind of future I'm facing?

My arm isn't right - of a twitch, I'm aware.
And my shoulder is aching due to wear and tear.

I've a bit of a rumble now on my left side
And my leg throbs like mad -this pain I can't abide.

I feel light headed, I'll have to get it controlled.
I'm sitting in the car because I'm feeling very cold.

The pain in my neck is due to whiplash, I guess.
I'll have to change my chair as it's causing distress.

I'm feeling hot and flustered and a little off key.
This long hot day is getting to me.

I've a nagging suspicion I could have gout
And I might have to have my gall bladder out.

I'm going for a lie down but don't worry, I'll be fine.
This is just a normal day for this body of mine.

THE MUSHROOM STORY

Yesterday a huge mushroom
Appeared on the chair.
It looked all forlorn
Just sitting there.

It was delivered by our neighbour,
A fungi to know.
He knows the difference between toadstools
And other things that grow.

It's many a year since
These presents first appeared.
We were younger then
Alarmed and somewhat feared!

We knew he picked them for his wife
A pretty lady with much class.
He fried them up with bacon
To give to his bonny lass.

So we watched and we waited
And kept the mushrooms for a day.
Then peeped over the fence
To make sure they were OK.

They must have had their mushrooms
At breakfast, we all knew.
And they still appeared cheerful
As good neighbours often do.

Our worries over,
We felt it was fine
To fry them with garlic
Olive oil and red wine.

This season has been plentiful,
With mushrooms by the score.
One mushroom in particular
Was bigger than our door.

So it is with many thanks
We say 'Please bring them when you can'
Now our caring, generous neighbour
Is known as 'The Mushroom Man'.

A SUMMER FLING

It really was quite ridiculous,
A sort of summer madness indeed.
It started with idle chatter,
But oh, how her eyes did plead.

He knew he was onto a good thing
And never even stopped to think,
Where, in the end this would all lead.
A thirsty dog never refuses a drink!

Before he knew it he was in too deep.
Oh, what a mess it had all become.
He didn't know which way to turn
When she said she was to become a mum!

He didn't need this aggravation
And was the child really his own?
His children were now all grown up
And from the nest, they'd recently flown.

His wife, she would go quite mental.
He contemplated suicide.
His car might have been a love boat
But he now surfed a very high tide.

How could it all have happened?
How could he have been so weak?
Everything in his life had been perfect,
And his career, it was at it's peak.

It was a moment of madness.
A very common human error.
He decided that night to tell his wife,
Though the thought of it filled him with terror.

DOWNHILL

Saggy boobs and droopy jowls,
Make-up put on with builders' trowels.
It's all downhill from here.

Blood shot eyes and wrinkles many,
Stay-young creams costing a pretty penny.
It's all downhill from here.

It's far too late for a tummy tuck
And a good facelift seems to be pot luck.
It's all downhill from here.

I look in the mirror and my mother looks back.
Will we die from a stroke or a heart attack?
It's all downhill from here.

The language has changed, it's a different era,
It wouldn't have done for my Auntie Vera.
It's all downhill from here.

The pension's low, it won't buy nowt,
My husband sits here and moans with his gout.
It's all downhill from here.
Oh, dear!

A SUMMER'S DAY

Cups and saucers on silver trays,
What better sight on sunny days?

Sat in the garden on the bench,
In the company of a sprightly wench.

I'll have some sugar, two lumps please.
Oh, you are a sweet little tease.

I'll chase you round the apple tree,
But only after I've taken tea.

These shortbread biscuits are divine,
Perhaps you'd like a drop of wine?

And another glass, maybe?
Yes, that's better…sod the tea.

Lets get merry in case we die,
Let not our life just pass us by.

Each second wasted is a loss,
Oh look! There goes an albatross.

Lets make hay whilst the sun doth shine,
Isn't life just *so* sublime?

THE WORLD TODAY

Unemployment, things are looking grim,
Wondering what's in life for him.
When he's searched his heart and soul
Next stop seems to be the dole.

People who had once known heroism,
Now face violence, death and terrorism.
The great big apple has turned rotten
And starving millions are still forgotten.

Love your neighbour and love his son,
Then tell your husband what you've done.
There are no laws to keep these days,
Nobody ever stops to pray.

Ban the bomb or bomb the moon.
Maybe that's what's coming soon.
Faceless people filled with greed,
Fighting only for their own need.

Nuclear energy and atomic war,
Wonder what we are here for?
If there's a God then we're in trouble,
We'd better start praying at the double.

DIAMOND LIL

She wears so much bling
It must weigh a ton,
I think they are gifts
From her famous son.

THIS DREAM OF A LIFE

Knobs and knockers and old broom handles,
Cabbages and kings and dimly lit candles.
Sausage and mash and cherry cake,
Are they for real, or simply just fake?

Buckets and spades and a seaside donkey,
Punch hit Judy and she felt quite wonky.
Father Christmas caused a sensation,
Just another figment of our imagination.

And so the fantasy goes on and on,
Clouds to built our life upon.
Keep optimistic and dare to dream,
Otherwise you might just scream.

❧

THE SPLIT

We see our Dad on Saturday,
He comes round once a week.
He sounds his horn outside our house,
Because he and Mum don't speak.

Ride this storm and calm will come,
After the rain there's always the sun.

Don't let your efforts go to waste,
Think things through, there is no haste.

What an empire you have made,
Don't let your love now start to fade.

Life is full of peaks and troughs,
Many a hiccup and plenty of coughs.

Love each other, please be strong
And soon you will be back on song.

EYE CONTACT

I've managed to make eye contact,
I think there's some interest there.
But I'm not sure how to make the next step,
'Cos they say of her – 'Just beware!'

LETTING GO

Mother could never understand,
How I wanted to just be me.
She always thought that I'd been influenced
By friends, with whom she didn't agree.

Mother could never accept
That I had a mind of my own.
That I so long yearned to develop
And escape the restraints I had known.

Mother was always disappointed
When I was old enough to want to break free.
It always really upset her
That she could no longer manipulate me.

All my life I have tried to cut loose
But events have just held me down.
Please write on my memorial stone,
'Free At Last To Paint The Town'.

CUCUMBERS

The salad days of youth,
The cucumbers I remember.
Especially one that comes to mind,
That grew in late September!

COUNTING THE COST

Nobody ever counts their pennies anymore,
Small change just doesn't matter.
The only sound to be heard at the till,
Is when the credit cards clatter.

Nobody minds being in debt now,
It doesn't have the stigma it had.
People just pay off their interest,
Which to me seems terribly sad.

Nobody really owns anything,
We all live in fantasy land.
It seems that as fast as we earn the money,
It slips through our fingers like sand.

Nobody is teaching prudence these days,
People think she's a fluffy black cat.
Well, we certainly need to have luck on our side,
Or a Daddy who's wallet is fat.

❧

SUMMER

It's cold and blowy tonight,
Cold enough to be the Fall!
The trees are shaking all around,
Elm trees and conifers tall.
What's happened to our summer nights?
It's the middle of August now.

CHIPS

Chips for supper, chips for tea.
Bread and Butter and chips for me.

Chips for breakfast, chips for lunch.
Forget bananas, even by the bunch.

Chips at snack time, chips for Lent,
Chips at Easter, I won't relent.

Chips in Summer, chips in Spring,
I just love chips more than anything.

Chips from McDonalds, chips at home.
Chips by the mirror as my hair I comb.

Chips in the hallway, chips on the loo.
I'm so full of chips, that there's chips in my pooh.

Chips and more chips, and more chips still.
Forget rabbit food, it just makes me ill.

Chips tomorrow, chips next week.
Chips by the mouthful, until I can't speak.

Chips to dream on, chips and peas.
I'd rather eat chips than watch a striptease.

Chips in my tummy, chips on my mind.
Chips by the plateful, all the chips I can find.

Chips forever, 'til the end of time,
I just think chips are so sublime.

AN ERRATIC MAN

His mind was so erratic
It bounced around at speed.
He could have been four people,
I kid you not indeed!

He could take on board so many things,
Most people would not need.
And store them in a secret box
As if he was planting seed.

His knowledge was so extensive,
An encyclopaedia in his head.
But his contrariness was really frustrating,
And quite often we'd all see *red!*

FASHION DIVA

I've got a lovely velvet coat,
It buttons to the floor.
I feel the bees knees in it.
But I don't wear it anymore.

I've got a heavy, thick black cape,
It comes right past my knees.
But I don't bother wearing it,
So my knees, I let them freeze!

I've got hundreds of matching suits,
That in my wardrobe sit.
But they are all last seasons,
And some, they don't even fit!

I've got four thousand pairs of shoes,
Some, I've never had on.
I've searched three months for my favourite pair,
I don't know where they've gone.

I've got millions of bottles of perfume,
Nail varnish and lipsticks too.
In every colour you can think of,
And guess what, I've even got blue!

You couldn't call me a hat chick,
So I thought I'd let you know,
That sitting in my cupboard
There's only ten or so.

I so love leather boots,
I admit I have a lot.
I feel so very sexy
When down the street I trot.

When it comes to cars,
I don't know why I've only got one!
I'll start a new collection,
Goodbye... I'm already gone...

࿓

UNREQUITED LOVE

Is it a fantasy that's got out of hand?
This crazy desire I can't understand?

Electric glances and silly flushed faces,
This sickly feeling as my heart races.

A secret longing, so ridiculous, it's untrue.
This frightening fear, when I'm close to you.

Weeks of nothing but contemplation,
A castle of dreams, without foundation.

A schoolboy crush, at my time of life!
When I was happy just being with my wife.

I must sort this madness in my head,
And finally put my desires to bed.

SHACKLES

Get me out of this pit of doom,
Set me free from the past.
Let me flee to pastures new,
Where I can breathe at last.

Let me walk alone, unaided,
Break these family shackles.
Let me see if I can cope,
When worldly things I tackle.

Treat me as an individual,
Let me be at peace,
Give me the confidence to make it happen,
All my baggage, please release.

THE FARM YARD

The corn fed chicken was free to roam
The farmyard paths that it called home.

The greedy pig used to like to scoff,
All the rubbish that was in the trough.

The gaggle of geese would stand so proud
But when they spoke, my God, they were loud.

The resident sheepdog was ever so bright,
He was the only one to see the light.

Old MacDonald had long since died,
'Not before time,' his wife she sighed.

The children had gone to pastures new
But the cows still stood there and sang with a moo.

The little old donkey in the far off grass
Backed up to the fence to scratch his ass.

The buttercups swayed in the gentle breeze
As the cat sat scratching away at its fleas.

Life seemed good, it was a normal day
As the farmhand romped away in the hay.

ROLE REVERSAL

Women are the new men
And who's to say they're wrong?
For too long men have had it all.
It's time for a brand new song.

Women will not be put on!
No longer will they be held down.
It's now the menfolk staying indoors,
Whilst the girls are out painting the town.

❧

SUDDEN DEATH

'Tis a nuisance when people die
Without a chance to say goodbye.
It makes me wonder if they died knowing
That they were loved as they were going.

In a normal day to day routine,
Our feelings seldom we reveal.
I suppose we all must feel reflective
When sudden death is so unexpected.

At any time our end could come
With so many jobs left still undone.
So let's enjoy life whilst we may,
Tomorrow might be our last day.

HIGH MORAL GROUND

High moral ground is a lonely plateau
Meant for the saintly few,
Who've never made a mistake in their lives,
And let's face it – are never likely to!

&

THE FORTUNE TELLER

A fortune teller once told me
That the worst day in my life had gone.
She was right of course and I knew it.
I have learnt how to carry on.

After that, other sadness was easy.
Though I felt in my heart quite upset.
For those people who now were grieving
But for me, the worst day I'd met.

It puts things in true perspective.
Yes, sorrow hardens the artery walls.
And places all other kinds of suffering
Into a box marked 'Unreturned Calls'.

Don't ever try to go there.
Just stick to the task ahead.
Get through the day the best way you can,
The worse day has gone, the gypsy said.

THE MAN WHO LIVED FOR NOW

He lived his life in the fast lane
On a road that had no hard shoulder.
He dashed around like Peter Pan
Not accepting he was getting any older.

He took unnecessary chances
Which really caused him more stress.
He never had anything in reserve
In case he ever got in a mess.

He sailed through life, as if on a cloud.
Always coming up smelling of flowers.
He lived each day as if his last,
Right up to his final hours.

DESIGNER GEAR

Bags in sumptuous leather,
Boots and shoes with a name.
All of them costing a fortune
Isn't it a shame!

Clothes with famous labels
Out of date so soon,
Get put on the credit card
And for the moment we're over the moon.

We all need 'retail therapy'.
To stop us going insane.
This fast track modern living
Can sometimes be a pain.

BELONGING

It takes a while
To really fit in
Before you feel
Content within.

It takes some time
To feel secure
And be at peace
And sure as sure.

Slowly, you will
Get to know
The people,
As they come and go.

Then one day,
The newness gone,
With your friends
You feel at one.

There'll be some,
More than others,
Who you'll feel,
Their friendship smothers.

So keep your counsel!
Be on your guard.
And soon they will hold you
In high regard.

ANXIETY

Why be anxious and anticipate
Why not just relax and wait.

The outcome won't be what you think,
So let your mind go on the blink.

Do not judge or indeed foresee,
Just think, 'What will be, will be.'

You cannot change a foregone conclusion,
So just imagine it's an illusion.

Most times anxiety is unfounded,
So let your feet stay firmly grounded.

No way can the past be changed,
Or the future re-arranged.

So just accept what's going on,
This time tomorrow, it will be gone.

Time doesn't wait, it never did,
So on anxiety, put the lid.

❧

UNEXPECTED GUESTS

Oh, goodness me,
They are coming to tea.
Why didn't they
Let me know?

Had I known, linen napkins
I could have pressed
And in my best clothes
I could have dressed.

They are quite welcome
But at their own cost.
Mum's frozen scones
I'll just have to defrost.

Patterned serviettes
Will have to do.
And I've run out of cream,
Oh, what a 't'do!

They rang on their mobile,
Those things I just hate.
Now ten minutes later
Their car's at my gate!

Oh, do come in darlings,
Quick, step out of the rain.
You must be frightfully hungry
Aren't people a PAIN!

People scurrying for the Tube,
During a working day.
Going about their business,
In their normal kind of way.

Rich and poor alike they weaved,
Through the bowels of the city.
Never knowing their fate that day,
Oh, God, it was a pity.

Innocent folks from far and wide,
It could have been you or me.
But we cannot walk on eggshells,
Nor into the minds of killers, see.

To read about it in the papers,
Brought sadness to our souls.
And to happen so soon after 'Live8',
Hampered our world peace goals.

We went from ecstasy into agony,
As we celebrated our Olympic bid.
It brought us back to reality,
Of terror – will we ever be rid?

But those precious family members,
Lost on the bus and the Underground
Will never be forgotten,
Whilst there's so much love still around.

REUNITED

A lovely lady with so much grace,
A smile for everyone upon her face.

A heart of gold and always cheery,
She did her best not to be weary.

A sense of humour that helped her through
The loss of her man, whom she loved so true.

Two brilliant children who did their best,
To help her survive life's toughest test.

A united family, seldom seen these days,
Of unity and love and caring ways.

A special person, no longer here,
And for whom we all will shed a tear.

A life not wasted for she's left behind,
Such memories of a special and tender kind.

Take strength, your Dad has paved the way,
To welcome his loved one home today.

Re-united.

DINNER PARTY

The atmosphere was very congenial,
The setting was really first class.
The host and hostess were hospitable
And gave us Champagne by the glass.

The menu was very imaginative,
Our chef was in cracking good form.
His friend Jerry Boam popped his cork,
But in the end he went down a storm.

The chef wore a 'Kiss Me Quick' pinny,
'Cos at his age it pays to beg
And we were all rather impressed
By his salad topped with quails egg.

One lady galloped off to the loo
Thirty four times whilst we dined!
She was supposed to be staying overnight,
The words 'rubber mattress' sprang to mind.

The food it just kept on coming,
We thought it would never stop.
And I swear that the kangaroo
At one point, even did a hop.

Then came the heavenly fruit
And all kinds of exotic cheese.
These really are gradely people
And certainly know how to please.

The same lady bombed off to the loo again,
The poor lamb needs incontinence knickers!
The candles were nearly burnt out,
And into their final flickers.

A blond guy was the first to look weary
And the hostess's eyelids started to drop.
Everyone, in turn, did a sneaky yawn,
So the party, finally had to stop.

It was a night to remember.
Though today, some might want to forget
As they crawl out from under the sheets,
En-route for the painkillers – you can bet!

&

COMPROMISE

We all put up with an awful lot,
In our daily attempt to survive.
We even deny our strongest beliefs,
When our confidence takes a dive.

Sometimes we have to rethink our thoughts,
In order to please our fellow man.
We all, in the end, must compromise,
To fit in with the master plan.

THE GRAND SLAM TOUR 2003

Saturday was a day to remember.
The Leader showed them the cultural scene,
Passing Bram Stoker's home
And then onto St. Stephens Green.

They stopped for a pint in the Shelbourne,
Then into Dublin's smallest drinking den.
Before finding a bar with a telly,
To watch the footy – well, men will be men!

The girls went off to do some shopping,
Saying 'Can we stay out 'till three?'
'Oh, yes,' cried the men with one voice,
While rubbing their hands with glee.

At last they could get down to business.
'Another six pints of Guinness, good man',
They shouted to the barman in eagerness.
'This draught sure beats that in a can!'

The girls arrived back at three twenty,
Thinking that they were so late.
But another game of footy had started,
So back out they went thinking, 'Great!'

At teatime they walked along Grafton Street,
And stopped at Bewleys Tea Place.
They ordered sandwiches and coffee,
The day was still picking up pace.

In the evening they went to the Guinea Pig,
Though they lost a 'big brother' on the way.
One guy was still feeling very sick
And decided to call it a day.

The men soon got talking politics
And the world's problems they did debate.
And decided to have some brandy,
When told that the taxi would be late.

Not realising they'd lose an hour
Next day, as the clocks were put on.
They headed to the bar for a nightcap,
But one jumped into the lift, and was gone.

The Leader had been promised tickets
From a guy, who'd never let him down.
They were to meet him in the second carriage
Of the next train heading for town.

This soon proved a journey to remember.
The passengers were crushed to bits,
One woman yelled: 'You're breaking my ribs!'
Another screamed: 'You're squashing my tits!'

Each time they pulled into a station
The doors slid open and still more got on.
One of the girls nearly burst into tears,
As sadly, her bottle had gone.

The Leader came good with the tickets,
Well, he got an all important two!
And with hindsight, for him and his best friend
It'd be a match they wouldn't want to view.

They'd probably have developed heart failure,
Or at least sunk into utter despair.
Because the game wasn't so much a 'walkover',
It was embarrassing beyond compare.

Two of them stood at the back of the stand
To avoid the inevitable squeeze.
Whilst another two headed towards The Herbert Park,
For stew and Guinness to at least appease.

Some headed into the city,
To find a livelier spot.
And stumbled up the stairs to O'Neills,
Into a room that was hotter than hot.

The sick guy was still feeling dodgy
And could have done with a place that was cool.
'I could give all this lot twenty years!'
He thought, as he stood on a stool.

But age, in the end, didn't matter.
As England won by a margin so clear.
And gave all the much travelled supporters
An excuse to down yet even more beer.

They then headed back to Mulligans
And ordered beers and coffees and coke.
And met one of the guys' older brothers,
Who turned out to be one hell of a bloke.

He was just back from touring Australia
And he had an amazing grin.
Due to a plate of teeth made from titanium
That he said was almost 'paper thin'.

The rest came in celebrating,
The unbelievable England win.
And really ribbed the Irish unmercifully
But they took it well, on the chin.

They all caught the train back to the hotel,
Including the brother and the best friend.
At least they could commiserate together,
'A sorrow shared' by good pals 'til the end.

The group then collected their cases.
Their adventure was over and done.
They all agreed the weekend had been terrific,
And best of all – England won!

AMBITION

Everything in moderation,
Our dear Dad always said.
But he worked 'til he was sixty five,
Then promptly dropped down dead.

Now where's the sense in that?

Just take this life steady,
Fit into the daily grind.
Don't be over ambitious,
Or indeed overstretch your mind.

Now where's the sense in that?

Just be Mister Average,
And follow the flock of sheep.
Tumble through life in wonderment,
As If you were half asleep.

Now where's the sense in that?

Dare to wake up feeling different.
With the blood running fast through your veins,
You can meet any challenge ahead,
If you'll only take hold of the reins!

Now there is some sense in *THAT!*

GETTING OLD

I can't recall from my memory bank
That incident of which you speak.
It mustn't have meant as much to me,
Unless, of course, I'm up the creek!

I can't recall from my mind's eye,
The person whom you remember.
But I think I met her sister once,
It could have been last September!

I can't recall from my book of life,
Most things of which you chatter.
Sometimes I think you've made them up,
But it doesn't really matter.

I can't recall from my many thoughts,
What I did a moment ago.
I've been looking all day for something I've lost,
But what it is, I'll never know!

ॐ

BONDAGE

The total complexity of marriage,
The unseen shackles that bind.
A lifetime sentence, after vows are exchanged,
We must be out of our minds!

PROPER FOOD

Suet pudding and Eccles cakes,
Oh, what goodies Grandma makes.

No ready meals in the microwave,
Just wholesome food, for which we rave.

No boil in a bag, or defrost is needed,
We asked for apple pie – in fact, we pleaded!

Coming through the door the aroma is divine,
And there's a pot of tea, but never any wine.

On Sundays she cooks beef or perhaps leg of lamb,
In the week she makes pea soup with a hock of ham.

She's plastered on the butter since I was at her knee,
How heart disease escapes her is a mystery to me!

It doesn't seem to harm the generation she came from
Once a year she visits Blackpool and strolls along the Prom.

Time to listen, she's never in a mood,
I love it at Grandma's 'cos she cooks real food.

Old fashioned values and home baked bread.
Followed by cocoa, taken to bed.

FIRST LOVE

Loves young yearning,
Her first romance,
A single kiss,
Her heart would dance.

Loves young sorrow.
Her first heartache,
In a single moment,
Her heart would break.

INHERITANCE

That pot of gold
Looks oh, so near.
But they don't go in hospital
To die now – no fear!

Don't count your chickens
Until they are here.
She might have left it
To the Dogs Home, Dear!

PONDERING

Pondering as I sometimes do,
I have to admit that I think of you
Just for a second, just for a minute.
It's just a dream, but you're always in it.

Always laughing, always fun,
Smiling in the summer sun.
Never far away from my thoughts are you.
You lift me when I'm feeling blue.

Flicking through my memory book,
It's nice at you to take a look.
It was sad at the end, though we gave it a try,
But it was always best we said goodbye.

❧

THE URGE

That sexual urge is back again
He *is* a persistent fellow!
You'd think that at his stage in life,
He'd be feeling a little more mellow!

TAKEN FOR GRANTED

He couldn't see the wood for the trees,
He'd got in far too deep.
His life had become a jungle
And at times he would sit and weep.

He couldn't break from the monotony,
He was on a conveyor belt.
His ambitions had long since left him,
All he had was the hand life had dealt.

His family took him for granted
And swallowed up all he could earn.
He even contemplated suicide,
He didn't know which way to turn.

In the end, one day he just walked off,
Sometime in the middle of May.
He took on another identity,
And found a new life, far away.

Nobody really missed him,
He should have done it long ago.
That's what happens when you're taken for granted.
Reality is a bitter blow.

THE WAIT

Whenever my daughter says she'll pick me up,
She's always half an hour late.
Sometimes I've finished my crossword,
Before she arrives at the gate!

OLD PALS ACT

As I entered the office I spotted it.
It really looked out of place.
It should have been a photo of his family,
But no, it was a familiar face!

There in a frame, for all to view,
In an unfortunate pose, gathering much moss.
Was a very unkind representation,
Of a man who used to be my boss.

A man not known for his dieting,
Nor for his choice in football teams.
But he was the best friend of this gentleman
In fact, they were both 'has-beens'.

One 'has been' to the conference
This year, like many years before.
The other 'has been ' on a diet,
Every year, for at least a score.

But two more genuine, gradely chaps
I don't think you ever could meet.
Their true camaraderie was legendary,
Yes, they really knew how to compete.

They both enjoyed different holidays,
You see one liked to sail on the sea.
The other was more into farming,
And said, 'Those waves just upset my tea'.

When it came to the game of football,
Once again, they couldn't agree!
One supported his local team,
The other said, 'Ee, lad, that's just not for me'.

They pulled each other's leg shamelessly,
And at times it caused great pain.
One wanted t'other to watch proper footy,
But his requests, were always in vain.

Great pals and stout fellows they still are.
A bit like Little and Large.
But the little'n still can't get his old mate
To sail on the Oriana Barge.

DEMENTED

Have you got the key or have I?
Did you lock up or me?
Is my handbag near the chair?
Where did I leave my cup of tea?

We're all going slowly crazy.
The pace of life, is too fast.
We're all heading towards dementia,
This nonsense cannot last.

LONELY HEARTS CLUB

I think I'll put an advert in
The 'lonely hearts' page today.
I need some feminine company
As none ever comes my way.

I can say that I am six foot two
When wearing my Cuban heeled shoes.
And put that I've got a GSH,
I think that's the language they use!

To say that I'm a 'professional' man,
Would be stretching the truth a bit.
So I'll put that I'm well educated
And that I'm slim and really fit.

I wonder if I should say I'm sporty
And into tennis and squash.
She's never likely to find out,
And it might attract a lady who's posh.

I'll say that I am only thirty eight,
With a lovely full head of hair.
Then meet her wearing my favourite hat
So she can't see there isn't any there.

I might as well say I love fast cars
And that I own one or two of those.
I'll also say that I'm good looking
Though I won't mention my very big nose.

I'll say I'm looking for a lady
Who's outlook is carefree and sunny.
Someone who is rich and slim,
Who's intelligent and also funny.

A lady who is about twenty five,
Or up to thirty at the most.
Someone who is good in the kitchen
And can cook a Sunday roast....!

On second thoughts, I'm going off the idea,
As nobody can cook like my Mum.
And girls today, they cost a fortune,
I'd have to be really dumb.

I'll have to go now, the bus is here,
And I've just dropped my walking stick
As I stood up in the bus shelter,
You see, these days, I'm not very quick!

෨

AGE OLD LAMENT

'It's not like it was in my day',
The old folks are heard to lament,
But *they're* not like they were in their day,
Life's disillusionments have left a dent!

Let the young enjoy their world,
Why not let them do it their way
Set them free to experiment,
After all, every dog has it's day.

YOUR GOAL

Don't lose sight of your objective,
There must be an end result.
Don't be lead by the nose,
Into the latest cult.

Just battle on and keep trying
Be original, don't be put off.
Try to ignore the cynics,
Even though they may laugh and scoff.

Shoot for goal and just keep focused,
Leapfrog over that five barred gate.
Determination won many a war,
Do it now before it's too late.

FEATHERS

Feathers floating through the air,
Your silky strands of sun kissed hair.
Such tender warmth, such feminine charm,
The sound of laughter through the calm.

The touch of your manicured fingers,
The fragrance of perfume still lingers.
Your gentle kiss, I more than miss,
Being with you was heavenly bliss.

Feathers floating through the air,
In case you're wondering –
I still care.

SIBLING RIVALRY

Look how successful I am today.
I saved all the money that came my way.

Look how successful I might have been,
If those opportunities I had seen.

Look how boring I have become,
I want for nothing – hey diddly dum.

Look how content I now feel,
I live in a world that's totally real.

Look how confused I am now,
As I gather much praise and take a bow.

All of my envy is now in the past,
Look how my sister needs me at last.

THE STRANGER

Touch the air he breathes,
It's impossible to do!

Feel the impression he's made
On everyone, not just you.

He is only passing by,
Let him go, from whence he came.

He never did belong here,
And he's surely not to blame.

MOTHER TO SON

What's the point of this debate?
You're in a contrary mood!
What's the point of this discussion?
If all you do is just brood!

What's the point of asking for suggestions?
When on them cold water you pour!
What's the point of me even speaking?
When you just barge out of the door.

What's the point of us carrying on?
We are never going to agree.
What's the point, I just can't win.
You're as awkward as awkward can be.

What's the point of being Mother and Son?
I wish that you'd outgrow this stage.
What's the point of asking my advice?
If my answer just fills you with rage?

What's the point of reaching your teens,
Just when I reach the menopause,
What's the point, I really don't know,
The path of life has its flaws.

What's the point - there must be a point!
I can't stand much more of you.
What's the point? Well, this is the point,
When you leave home I know I'll feel blue.

SON TO MOTHER

Don't try to tell me just what to say,
I surely know my own mind!
Don't lead me up your path of life,
My own route I must find.

Don't manipulate, just let me go free,
And then you'll find that we'll agree.
Please don't nag when I get in a mood,
Just let me be.

Release me from your apron strings,
So less pressure I feel.
Try to understand the way that I am,
Then more love I'll reveal.

You are the best Mum, but give me some space,
You'll find that I won't disappoint.
You've been just great, now it's time for me,
I love you tons – have I made my point?

❧

FLIRTING

I believe we have unfinished business,
That's been hanging around for years.
Odds and ends that should be tied up,
So get up those apples and pears!

WORKING FROM HOME

The idea of him working from home,
Initially, did seem great.
But to date it's been a disaster,
Because my partner likes to delegate.

'Just get me this', or 'Go and fetch that',
Are just two of his constant demands.
He thinks I should stand to attention,
Whenever he claps his hands.

'I'll have a drink, if you're making one',
Or 'A spot of lunch would be nice'.
'Oh, and could you renew my prescription?
And put my Champagne on ice?'

Well, enough is enough, and I told him so!
I said, 'Be off and don't come back
Until you've learnt how to treat a wife properly.
And with that, his briefcase, he packed.

He fled through the door like a madman,
With steam coming out of his ears.
No doubt, on the way back from the meeting,
Before he greets me, he'll need a few beers.

But I think he'll be glad to see me,
And I know I'll be glad when he's in.
We'll soon relax into a routine,
And 'The Office at Home' war, we'll win.

MORE RAIN

Here comes the promised rain,
What a pain!
We mustn't grumble or get upset,
At least we're indoors and we aren't wet.

Gone are the cobwebs that looked like spun lace,
Gone forever, without a trace.
The spiders have vanished, both big and small.
Except for the one on the rug in the hall.

Up comes the grass that we mowed yesterday,
Becoming tomorrow's bundles of hay.
It's a vicious circle, round and round,
Faster, faster, out of the ground.

Here come the birds, magpies and crows,
Searching for worms and whatever else grows.
The sparrow thinks he has found a winner,
But the tomcat too, has seen his dinner.

It's the law of the jungle,
Let's eat each other.
What else can we do,
When it's raining…bother!

❦

DESPAIR

The pain of death is so hard to bear,
Knowing you are no longer there.
Just a hollow emptiness
And utter despair.
No point in carrying on.

The things we did, the life we had.
We saw it through both good and bad.
Just a broken heart,
So very sad.
No point in carrying on.

I cannot handle this sudden life change.
My affairs I just can't rearrange.
Just a pointless void,
I feel so strange.
No point in carrying on.

They say in time I will feel better.
That I should sit and write a letter.
But, I was dead
Before I met her.
No point in carrying on.

We were soul mates in every sense.
Though that is still no recompense.
In fact it's worse, from here on, hence,
No point in carrying on.

Today I think I can begin.
I've even put aside the gin.
This self indulgence
Is a sin.
Some point in carrying on.

DECISION TIME

The leaves are turning brown and your love's fading,
Let's talk this thing out and stop masquerading.
I'd rather live without you, than see you looking blue,
It's affecting all of us, not just you!

You cannot look straight at me,
You know that I know you too well.
I see you watch the children,
You must be going through hell.

I don't want you to stay, for the childrens' sake.
For every day you'd feel resentment and strain.
Because you'd decided to stay, against your will,
Still, it's your decision now.

Go to her if she's right for you,
But I won't have you back, if you do.
It's up to you!

The leaves have fallen to the ground,
And as I look around,
My love has finally gone,
But peace, at last, I've found.

MAGICAL CATS

I saw a cat with bright green eyes,
Down at the Rescue today.
He looked at me and said, 'Take me home,
Would I just, if I'd had my own way.

I saw a lovely tabby mum,
With her two sons – Fluffy and Felix.
They tore at my heart but I already have four
And with them they would just never mix.

I saw other cats trotting here and there.
Going about their daily routine.
The feeling down there is beyond compare,
It's the best place I've ever been.

I've been to Paris and London too
And I've drank Champagne on a boat.
But a visit to the Cat Rescue Home
Always brings a lump to my throat.

There's something down there, so tranquil and still.
Simply something that money can't buy.
I could bring them ALL home but my husband said NO!
Ah, well, it was still worth a try!

Some cats are majestic, others are bold
And some just know how to charm.
All cats are wise and give out much love,
Just one stroke brings so much inner calm.

If you feel you could sponsor a lonely cat
That's been abandoned, or simply is lost.
It's the most worthwhile thing you ever could do,
No matter how little the cost.

These creatures are mystical, we need them around
To make sense of this crazy old planet.
It can't hurt to love them and give them a home.
Well, really, I ask you, can it?

WEARY (BUT WAIT!)

I really am quite weary,
In fact I feel ready to die.
All of life's excitement
Now seems to pass me by.

I can't get enthusiastic,
I no longer think life's a ball.
And I wouldn't want to be a burden,
That wouldn't be right at all.

It's not the same since my love went,
And crossed to the other side.
I coped rather well at first,
But then I let things slide.

I got behind with my polishing,
And I couldn't be bothered to cook.
I even stopped visiting the hairdresser,
And I lost interest in my library book.

I feel I'm no longer useful,
Nobody wants my advice or my time.
I just stay indoors recalling,
How life used to be so sublime.

I don't think I'd want another man
There's no time to break him in!
And you have to be very careful,
You might just get one who drinks gin.

There's a lady just moved in next to me,
Her husband died only last week.
We've waved and smiled at each other,
But we haven't had chance yet to speak.

She looks a very nice person,
So smart and very refined.
I think I'd better ring my hairdresser,
If only his card I could find.

I'll give the house a 'once over',
In case she wants to come in.
And I'll get a bottle of sherry,
On her face, that should put a grin!

I hope she's got plenty of money!
I might ask her to go on a cruise.
Once we become firm friends,
We can do whatever we choose.

We wouldn't go chasing men,
Nor give them a second glance,
We would have a session of bingo,
And join in the daily line dance.

It's not the same with my love gone,
But I'm learning to carry on.
We all seem to live longer now,
Next month I'll be ninety one.

❧

THE FACELIFT

Improve your look, renovate your face,
Have plastic surgery, just in case.

Your crows feet are now growing toes,
Don't go outside when the cold wind blows.

Conceal your past, cleanse your mind,
The new you is here – and oh, so refined.

Recycle your thoughts, yesterday doesn't matter,
You can't join in any wartime chatter!

Look in the mirror, are you still there?
Oh, my God, there's some grey in your hair!

Your laughter lines have gone under the knife,
And the heart bypass should extend your life.

But tell me truly, what is the point!
With arthritis creeping into every joint.

You're bottom is sagging and to tell you straight,
You seem to me to be overweight!

You look like an oddity, something's not right.
What on earth do you see, when you undress at night?

SCEPTICISM

A world full of contradictions
And double standards by the score.
White lies are ten a penny.
Truth matters not anymore.

ॐ

MUCH TOO YOUNG

Go away, you are much too young for me,
You're asking for trouble, just you see!
It's fun to flirt, until someone gets hurt,
So please, just go away from me.

I know older women you find more appealing,
You say they make love with a lot more feeling.
I know you're passionate, I've heard you talk,
But for your sake now – little boy – just walk!

I felt it the first time I touched your hand,
That sexual attraction that nobody planned.
So I'm begging you to just leave through that door,
As I'm finding this feeling so hard to ignore.

Please go now, you're too much to resist,
I've known it ever since the first time we kissed.
But if in your mind you're really quite certain,
Then you go upstairs, whilst I draw the curtain.....

THE INVITATION

Would you like to come for lunch?
I do a lovely Bakewell Crunch.

Would you like to come for dinner?
My tender lamb, it is a winner.

Would you care to take some wine?
I have a red that's quite divine.

Would you like some coffee roasted?
And some crumpets, I have toasted?

Would you like to have a chat?
I really rather fancy that.

If my offer you do turn down,
Then I will surely have a frown.

You'd be a fool, the offers good,
And on the fire, there'd be some wood.

The company would be so charming,
Just thee and me…. is that alarming?

Well, I'll leave you now to ponder,
As I gaze at the rainbow over yonder.

THE BREAD WINNER

The pressure of being the bread winner,
Has unforeseen stress of it's own.
The family are so very demanding,
So we take out loan after loan.

The children always seem to need something,
That they've seen advertised on TV.
So that means working longer hours,
Then my wife gets mad when she doesn't see me.

We are caught in a vicious circle,
It's just a roundabout of life.
And the pressure builds up so silently,
'Til the heart attack stabs like a knife!

≈

PMT

When the balance of the mind untips,
And words not meant are on our lips,
And museum archives get trotted out,
It's that time of the month again!

LIFE MUST GO ON

My children have all grown up now,
And fled the nest long ago,
Some stayed single and travelled,
It was hard when they had to go.

Others got married and had children,
Though they are divorced now, it's true.
They didn't try to hold things together,
Well, that's my own personal view.

My husband, he died last summer,
He wasn't the love of my life.
But we settled for what we had,
And I think I made him a good wife.

My grandchildren rarely visit,
They think I'm on another planet,
The generation gap has widened somewhat,
Thanks to the computer age – damn it!

We all seem to need our own space now,
We all want to do our own thing.
My eldest son popped in last week,
And declared that he's had a 'gay fling'.

It certainly didn't surprise me,
Nor did it cause me dismay,
I love all my children, whatever they do,
And they must get through life their own way.

Well, I think that I'd better get ready,
I'm being picked up at half past seven.
I dare not tell my children my secret,
But I've found a man who's just heaven.

EXAGGERATION

Did he see THREE or was it FOUR?
Well, that's not what he said before!

He told me that he'd seen SEVEN,
But he told Ted that it was ELEVEN,

He said to Hazel that it was TEN,
He must have changed his mind again!

Shall we come to this conclusion,
That it was a grand illusion?

Or perhaps he actually did see ONE,
That he based his tale upon.

Let's not leave him feeling blue,
Let's just say, 'He saw a few'!

Let us not his confidence shatter,
All in all, it doesn't matter.

Just look amazed, heaven forbid,
Even if he never did!

THE EARLY RISER

What do you make of an early riser,
Who gets up at 4.30 in the morning?
He anticipates the day ahead,
Long before it's actually dawning!

To him life is one big adventure,
Each new day brings with it a thrill.
His enthusiasm has sent folks quite mad,
Some have even slipped him a sleeping pill!

Today he's excited and really eager to go,
And says, 'Let's get up now and be gone!,
This English climate is fickle you know,
Please get out of bed now, dear one.'

But his partner is alarmed
And somewhat perplexed.
And to be perfectly honest,
A little bit vexed!

What time is it now?
This is really insane!
The cup of tea is nice,
But you really are a pain!

With a push and a shove,
He lands on the floor,
Rubbing his tender parts,
Gosh, they're sore!

'Where is it we're going?
What time is the train?
No, I haven't seen the brolly,
Do you think it will rain?'

He turned to him, crossly,
'I'll remind you tonight,
When you're sleepy and grumpy,
And *so* out of fight!

'And battling to keep
Your eyelids from shutting
When on the dance floor
They're still jumping and strutting.

Then maybe, just maybe, the day will catch up
On the one of us who was making a cup
Of tea, in the hours that God made to rest
For thee and for me, so don't be a pest!'

You can't burn the candle at both ends dear boy,
So sleep while you may and be filled with joy.
For each day that dawns is a bonus indeed,
But to rise before the sun, is a sin, so I plead.

That next time you wake early.
Quietly open the lock,
And take yourself off,
For a walk around the block.

Or go to the park,
Or over yonder heights,
Because, man of mine,
I must sleep at nights.

MR. GREEDY

His eyes were bigger than his tummy,
His greed I did deplore,
Just like Oliver Twist,
He always wanted more.

Whatever was on offer,
He would merrily devour,
A faster eater there never was,
No chance of it turning sour!

I don't know where he put it.
To watch him made me heave,
And often from his table,
I simply had to leave.

He would have the Champagne starter,
And canapes by the score,
And then the soup and fish course,
And still shout, 'More, more more!'

He would polish off his roast beef,
And Yorkshire pudding too.
Then onto the sweet trolley,
His hungry eyes would glue.

I don't know where he put it,
To watch him made me ill.
Quite often he would need
An indigestion pill.

He doesn't eat so much these days,
I think he's slowing down,
He rarely has three courses,
Unless he's been out on the town.

He cannot seem to get his breath,
He puffs and pants at leisure.
Never did I see anyone
From ice cream get such pleasure!

અ

KEEP IT INSIDE
————————————

Don't let all the people know,
Your every waking plan,
Keep a little inside,
Whenever you possibly can.

It's one thing being honest,
But don't give the game away.
Being an open book,
Doesn't always pay.

Best to keep a bit inside,
And have something in reserve.
Or others will steal from under your nose,
Some people do have a nerve!

WORKING WEEK

I've just got back from the office,
My day, it's been just hell.
I've had to sack three salesmen,
They simply didn't know how to sell.

The pressure was on me to do it,
Though they are all really decent chaps.
But the figures just weren't adding up,
And we couldn't see the firm collapse.

Tomorrow I'm back on the road,
Off, up to the Highlands again.
Motorway road works will slow me down,
And the forecast is torrential rain.

There's no easy way of earning a living,
So I must press on and secure the next deal.
If only my family would understand,
When I walk through the door, how I feel!

OLD ENGLAND

Old English traditions ,
Like home made jam
Period cottages
And sugar baked ham.

Long, sleepy Sundays,
Tender roast beef.
England, my England
Oh, what a relief.

FRIEND

In our lives we have lots of pals,
And acquaintances by the score.
I don't suppose that we ever know,
Which of those we really bore.

But how many people
Can we really call our friend?
Who'll support us through thick and thin
Right to the end?

A real friend will tell us that we are wrong,
Knowing that we will shout.
They'd rather be truthful and make us see sense,
Than see us look a fool – I've no doubt.

A friend can be candid but still remain loyal.
And at times drive us right round the bend.
But they'll always listen at the drop of a hat,
And always our problems they'll mend.

A true friend is priceless
A solid rock,
Upon whom we can always depend.

෴

WEEKEND

Let's sink a few pints in the bar tonight
And breathe in that thick smoky air.
Let's follow them up with some chasers,
Brandy, or whisky.....who cares?

Let's all get legless and abusive,
And chant to our heart's content.
And on the way home have a curry,
And say what a good night we've spent.

Tomorrow we're out at the football match,
But we meet at the pub for twelve.
And sink three more pints, ah, that's better!
Again, into our pockets we delve.

I think I might have a pork pie,
Or maybe I might even have two.
That should take me up to half time,
When I'll have two more pints – it's true!

I probably won't know what the result is,
When the game finally comes to a close.
I usually nod off in the second half
And have a bit of a doze.

On the way home I pass the hot dog stand,
And I normally have two of those.
They set me up for the night you see,
A Saturday night on the town.

When I'll probably have a pint of Guinness,
Or maybe a Newky Brown,
I always have a bag of pork scratchings,
And another pint to wash them down.

Then I might have a Baileys chaser,
If I get into that kind of mood.
Before I call off at the Chippy,
Oh, how I do love my food.

Last week when I ambled home,
I was glad to reach our gate.
I had such pains in my arms and chest,
I think it was something I ate!

Sunday lunch at the pub is just great,
We take bets who can down the most.
I'd tell you that I always win,
But I really don't want to boast.

These pains in my chest have come back,
And I can't seem to get rid of this cough.
I'm just out to have my last supper,
Before they carry me off.

THE ARRIVAL

Fields of clover growing wild,
The piercing scream of a newborn child.
What a time she chose to arrive,
How is she ever going to survive?

The peace we know will soon just shatter,
As Heads of State commence their chatter.
Wise words spoken – we must attack.
We're in too deep to now turn back.

Freedom we just took for granted,
Our look at life was always slanted.
Complacent we had all become
After the Second World War was won.

Ambition and greed and selfish ways!
No wonder the willow tree sadly sways.
We always thought that we'd be free,
But hell is coming to earth – you'll see.

IMPRISONED

Remorse, regret, suffering yet.
The future is just a haze.
Totally trapped, locked in the past,
Recalling much happier days.

SWEET AND SOUR

The perfume of a rose,
That lingers,
Long after the thorn
Has pricked your finger.

Oh, for the sweet and sour.

The romantic sound,
Of a soulful singer.
Turns to heartache,
When he doesn't linger.

Oh, for the sweet and sour.

An intimate picnic,
On a sunny day.
Is washed away,
By the rain in May.

Oh, for the sweet and sour.

That incredible passion,
That makes your heart go ping.
Is wiped out when
His wife he must ring.

Oh, for the sweet and sour.

WISHING TIME AWAY

We are always wishing time away,
We should learn to live for now,
And treasure every moment,
The best way we know how.

We are always wanting something,
That's just a little bit out of reach.
Like a wonderful, dreamy holiday,
On a far off Caribbean beach.

We are rarely ever grateful,
Or content with what we've got.
We are all just media junkies,
Giving in to temptation's plot.

OUR SON

The pain will never go away,
But his memory we still hold dear.
And when we pause to think of him,
He seems so very near.

It was a joy to know him,
Though briefly, he did stay.
He's still a part of our family,
And will always remain that way.

His smile was easy – I can see it now,
So clear, in my mind's eye.
I live each day with one regret,
That we never said Goodbye.

OLD FRIENDS

It was never really over,
For there never was an end.
In a crisis they would get in touch,
They were still each other's friend.

It wasn't really unfinished business.
For sex had long since gone.
It was nice to have someone out there,
They could sometimes lean upon.

To meet would be foolhardy,
To love would be insane.
It's a mistake in life to ever go back
For it always ends in pain.

But it's nice to chat, every now and then
And bring each other up to date.
Who knows what the future holds for them
For no one knows their fate!

FAMILY ADVICE

You silly little fool,
Why didn't you come and tell me.
I could have helped you out,
And shared the pain.

Fancy keeping it to yourself.
Why didn't you seek advice?
They would have sorted you out,
And eased the strain.

GARDENING

I might just go hedge cutting up the lane,
Those overgrown branches drive me insane.

It seems that I cut them only last week,
They must have grown an inch as I speak.

My biggest nightmare is that Russian Vine,
As the resident gardener, I think I'll resign!

The snails have chewed up all my plants,
And the flower tubs now are full of ants.

My clever friend who's hot in the grass,
Said 'Get some bone meal'.....Ee what a lass!

She's full of information, always ready to please.
It was her who told me it gets hot in marquees.

Her garden is perfection, a landscape dream.
Not a petal out of place, it makes me want to scream.

I guess some of us are born with natural green fingers,
While others turn out to be church bell ringers.

What joy it must be, just playing cricket.
But for me, well, I'll just return to the thicket.

I'll just tidy up and keep things neat,
'Cos as a rose pruner, I'll accept defeat.

PASHMINAS

Heather appeals to my sense of calm,
Like pale blue water, it has its charm.

Raspberry Ripple just sends me wild,
With pale fuschia petals, ever so mild.

Lavender too, is so very gentle,
It calms me down when I feel mental.

Persian Prince with Arab descent,
In royal blue is heaven sent.

Blushing Bride, wearing just pale pink!
Why not white, it makes me think.

Silver Cloud that has no lining,
In soft grey, would have me whining.

Angora Cream, well, what a delight,
A cashmere dream, to cuddle at night.

Simply Taupe, so plain and dull,
Not a red rag to a bull.

Bright Red it could never be,
Not for you, and not for me.

NEVER NUMBER ONE

He couldn't help the way he was,
He'd never been number one.
He was the middle one of five,
And nobody thought he shone.

He couldn't help the way he felt.
He'd never been looked upon,
As anyone kind of special,
No one's confidence had he won.

He couldn't help the way he fought.
His anger was deep within.
No one had ever taken the time,
To get to know the real him.

He couldn't help the way he loved,
His new bride, she'd shown him new hope.
He was number one with someone at last
And she had taught him how to cope.

He couldn't help the way he saw
The birth of his new born son.
He couldn't come to terms with the fact
That he was no longer number one.

He couldn't help the way he felt,
His loneliness was back once more.
His wife now slept in another room,
She couldn't stand to hear him snore.

He couldn't help the way he was
Life's lottery had dealt a cruel hand
He just needed to be number one,
Didn't anyone understand!

FAMILY CHANGES

I'm going through a midlife crisis,
They all said that it would appear
When the children went to university,
And the dog died who was most dear.

At the same time I lost my mother.
And my father-in-law went round the bend.
Leaving me alone with his wife and son,
Will this nightmare just never end?

We've now got a leaking ceiling,
And the cat has been missing for days.
I've so far resisted the bottle,
But my mind is lost in a haze!

I'll have to re-think my future,
I think it is time for pastures new.
I need a mental clearout,
So I can get a more balanced view.

᷃

TRIUMPH OVER ADVERSITY

I love to sit and read a book
In the tranquillity of my home,
Amongst familiar surroundings,
And tomorrow I might fly off to Rome.

It's up to me, Don't you agree?

I love to take a leisurely bath,
And sigh with satisfaction,
At having raised four lovely kids,
In spite of negative reaction.

As you can see, I'm filled with glee!

I 'earned' this status, that I've now reached
And if others, through envy, turn green.
I cannot be blamed for their failings,
But I do think their comments are mean.

Oh, fiddle de dee, they don't worry me.

I let so much go over my head.
But at times I could say more.
Which would no doubt stir up a hornet's nest
And probably have them slamming the door.

So I let it be, Well you know – that's me!

But what goes around, will come around again.
So I'll sit and bide my time.
And just carry on enjoying my life,
And with two fingers, I'll end this rhyme.

In the sign of a 'Vee' – Don't you agree?

ॐ

MOVE ON

Take what he gave you,
His knowledge and his care,
And move on.

Take what he taught you,
His wisdom and truth,
And move on.

Take what he showed you,
His warmth and his love,
And move on.

Take what he left you,
Tomorrow and the future.
So move on.

MEMORY LANE

The farmlands of England,
Rich and green,
Where as a girl
I played so serene.

The simple walks,
For miles and miles,
Under arches
And over stiles.

My Uncle Bob and
His brother Bill,
Who owned the farm
At the top of the hill.

They bought me a pup
Named 'Devil's Herd',
My Mother said 'No',
It looks absurd!

So they took it home
Which made Mum merrier.
She said it looked like a pig,
Not an English bull terrier.

I remember the see-saw
And swings in the park,
Where we played for hours,
Just having a lark.

Safe as houses,
Not like today,
Though Johnnie Pac-a-mac,
Once flashed our way!

We ran home as fast
As our legs were able.
The police got him next day,
And that's no fable.

In those days policemen
Walked the street.
It seemed back then,
Crime was easy to beat.

Innocent times,
In the woods all day.
Swinging on a rope
And not a penny to pay.

Making secret tents
Under the table in the front room,
We'd sit and laugh for hours,
It was our own little tomb.

Playing jacks and marbles,
And hop scotch in the street.
And if someone had a bike,
Well, that was a proper treat.

Lovely cosy memories
Of carefree childhood days,
Still give me such pleasure
In so very many ways.

ALCOHOLISM

I could take on the world but what's the use
Of all this fighting and abuse?
I might just do it in a minute.

I could escape to a world and never come back,
Or even die from a heart attack.
I might just do it in a minute.

I could linger a while, in some back alley,
Grinning inanely and acting pally.
I might just do it in a minute.

I could be King Kong and beat my chest
On top of a building, away from the rest.
I might just do it in a minute.

I could slump to the floor where I've been before
And ask forgiveness just once more.
I might just do it in a minute.

I could book myself into a rehab place
And once again look myself in the face.
I might just do it in a minute.

I could rediscover my self-esteem
And turn this nightmare into a dream.
I might just do it in a minute.

I could go to sleep for a million years
Because no-one out there really cares.
I might just do it in a minute.

SOME OF US

We all expect to wake up every day,
But some of us won't.

We all think that we'll still be here tomorrow ,
But some of us won't

We all expect to sometime fall in love,
But some of us won't.

We all think we'll stay married forever more,
But some of us wont.

We all expect to tread life's normal path,
But some of us won't.

We all think we'll have children too someday,
But some of us won't.

We all expect to see a silver lining,
But some of us won't.

We all think that we'll someday go to heaven,
But some of us won't.

THE DICTATOR

He ruled the conversation,
On and on for hours he chattered.
He loved the sound of his own voice,
No-one else's opinions mattered.

ABSENT FRIEND

I like you enormously,
I think you know that's true,
Although it is a long time,
Since we sat down for a brew!

Time goes by so quickly,
But I've long had you in mind,
You are the sweetest peach
That anyone could find.

Months went by and turned into a year,
And the longer I left it, the guiltier I felt.
To tell the truth, I was scared to see you,
In case I got a belt!

So let us put the matter right,
And get together real soon.
Or else before we know it
We'll find ourselves in flamin' June!

Let me know when it's convenient,
And I'll write the date down.
Mid-week would suit me best
We'll go and paint the town!

HATRED

How are we ever going to exist together
If the sins of our fathers we can't forgive?
Generations still hating with a passion,
What a cancerous way to live.

INEVITABILITY

Steely grit and determination,
Will surely help us through.
Innocent people will suffer,
Whatever are we going to do?

WHOSE HOUSE IS IT ANYWAY?

The meaning of life,
A romantic night.
The kids are now grown,
So we're out for a bite.

The meaning of life,
A walk through the park,
And on the way home,
A kiss in the dark.

The meaning of life,
Our home's been attached.
Our son's brought his friends,
And the place – it's just packed!

The meaning of life,
I'm still a fit lass.
So on the way home,
A romp in the grass.

The meaning of life,
The pendulum swings.
There's still so much joy,
That living can bring.

POST BOX

I saw it leave my fingers,
I even heard it drop
Into the empty post box.
My life had been a flop.

I had to admit defeat,
I had to get away.
I rushed off down the street,
To start a new life on that day.

Looking back, I was half crazy.
It was as if it wasn't me.
I actually made something happen,
Instead of 'What will be, will be!'

It must have been survival.
A case of 'I've really had enough'.
I had to have a life change,
On myself I was quite tough.

Sometimes, in life, there's a moment.
That forever springs to mind.
For me it was posting that letter,
So that a better life I could find.

MENAGE A TROIS

Beyond the realms of acceptance,
The three of them that night explored!
It was the craziest thing they could do,
But raw passion just can't be ignored.

THE GREATEST GIFT

The body you inherit
When you come onto this earth,
Is the only one you'll ever have,
So cherish it from birth.

The life you are beginning,
When you come into this land.
Is the greatest gift you'll ever have,
A world of knowledge to command.

But remember it's your only one,
You won't ever have another.
So treat it with respect and care,
Yes, take the time to bother.

Enjoy each passing hour,
And make the most of every day.
Or else this life will just have been,
A waste – in every way.

THE BEST

She couldn't bear to see him go,
She knew it was forever.
But better still to have had the best.
Much better, yes than never!

FINALITY

I never knew that morning that your last breath was so near.
It happened so suddenly and it haunts me, Mother Dear.
It seems that you were needed in a better world than this,
God's angel had a mission, to find a 'classy Miss'.

His brief was very simple. 'Bring me someone kind,
'Someone who has done life's task and can leave her family
behind,
'A lady who sees beauty, in flowers and birds and trees'.
Mum you readily volunteered, as you slid down to your
knees.

I knew the call was urgent, the moment was so swift.
You were already on your journey, as your body I tried to lift.
I now feel ready to move on, knowing that you are there,
Sitting by the side of Dad – in his loving care.

Thanks for all the values you taught us every day.
Goodbye our lovely Mother, God speed you on your way.
Time has a nasty habit of never standing still.
But our thoughts are with you always, well, you know,
until…..

GROWING UP

We don't grow up, we just grow wiser,
And give ourselves a break.
We just move on, we learn some sense,
For everybody's sake.

ASSERTION

Reluctantly, I have to say,
That I really couldn't possibly do it.

Unfortunately, I won't be here,
I'm unavailable, I just blew it!

Desperately, my diary is full.
But your invitation was *so* kind.

Frustratingly, I'm well over-booked,
But next year, please keep me in mind.

The simple truth is, I don't want to do it.
No way, whatever the fee.

The way I feel now, it wouldn't be right,
So it's no use relying on me.

I'd just sooner not bother, it's not my cup of tea,
There, I've said it, what a load off my mind!

By the way, next year, just forget I exist,
Though to ask me was awfully kind!

HOPES

If only we had the courage of conviction.
If only we had the strength
To put into practice our dreams and desires,
That we harp on about at great length.

THERE'S ALWAYS TOMORROW

It doesn't really matter,
If the job is not quite done.
We can finish it tomorrow,
At our leisure in the sun.

CHANCE MEETING

Far into the future,
Caught quite unaware,
One day at your face,
I will suddenly stare.

Perhaps at the opera,
Or even at the races.
Galloping hearts,
And red blushing faces.

Feelings still there,
Suppressed through the years.
Scary thoughts indeed
And with them - come tears.

THAT UNMENTIONABLE BIRTHDAY

I'm sorry your birthday came and went
Before this card from me was sent.
It's not that I'm idle or even slow,
But honestly darling, I just didn't know.

Age matters not, it's only a number.
So try to relax and on your eyes put cucumber.
Have reflexology on those busy feet,
And support your back with a new office seat.

Just do what you want, now you're getting the pension,
Oop's there I go, another word not to mention.
It's many a year since I first met you,
Some laughs we've had and a tear or two.

But you'll get your revenge, because I'm not far behind
That horrible number, that makes us all blind.
The best of life is wished for you,
And to me you'll always be thirty two.

PEOPLE

People are people,
The whole world over.
The poor they long for,
A four leafed clover.

The rich are still searching,
For they know now,
That happiness and health
Can't be bought anyhow.

FRIDAY AT ASCOT

The weather at Ascot had been mixed all week
And Ladies Day was no exception.
So they felt very lucky to land a sunny Friday
For the traditional yearly reception.

The ladies looked terrific and were in good spirits
And they got some hints on studying form
From the professional help of a tipster,
Who really went down a storm.

The canapés arrived and the Champagne flowed
And then they all sat down to eat.
The pudding came at the same time as The Queen
So they all quickly leapt to their feet.

The excitement grew as the first race neared
And they felt sure that they'd picked a winner!
But alas, an outsider flew past the post
Making their wallets just that little bit thinner.

With Placepots down the drain
They quickly moved on to the second race of the day.
Some strolled to the paddock and mingled with the crowd
And soaked up the merriment on their way.

As the day progressed they all seemed to get luckier,
Well, of one table that was certainly true.
As someone won Champagne in the Sweep
And the second prize came their way too!

The Queen didn't get a chance to pop across
And chat to them over afternoon tea.
But they knew she was tied up in the Royal Box
So they just had to let things be.

As the last race neared, it was a chance to win back
Some of the money that had been lost.
But being a 'Bumper' – a donkey won
And they all shook their heads, to their cost.

Then all too soon it was over
And they felt a little bit sad
As they gathered to say their goodbyes
And hoped that the traffic wasn't bad.

REMEMBER

Remember when times were exciting
With no responsibilities to dwell upon?
When the only thing that seemed important
Was whether the sun came out and shone.

Remember feeling so very carefree?
When time was really our own.
No hassle, no rush, no commitment.
No, not even a mobile phone.

Remember when things really mattered?
And somehow people always had time.
When folks left their front doors open,
Without any fear of crime.

Remember those long gone days?
When people weren't in search of power.
And time just used to tick by,
Gently, hour by hour.

Remember when life was so simple?
When selfishness and greed were rare.
When people looked after each other,
And were always willing to share.

Remember, remember, remember.
For those times are a far off planet.
That has long since, sadly, uprooted.
And left us forever, damn it!

HUMAN ERRORS

I often wonder if I was a mistake.
The product of a night of passion.
When everything was in short supply
And love on the dole was the 'fashion'.

I always own up to the smallest mistake.
Because not to, would only be folly.
If sorry doesn't work, then plead insanity.
It's OK to be quite off your trolley!

It's best to recover from any such mistake,
As fast as you possibly can.
Get it right off your chest and lay it to rest
And move on to your very next plan.

As we all grow, we must make that mistake,
From which we always step back and retreat.
How many times must we wobble and fall.
Before finally finding our feet?

How dull life would be without a single mistake
To refer to at some later stage.
And how sad not to have in our memory bank
A mistake that was worth a week's wage!

❧

THE APPLE TREE

The single apple
Looks so lonely.
It needs a friend,
A 'one and only'.

Some were taken
And others fell.
Perhaps by Eve,
Who can tell?

Some with grubs,
Now lay rotten.
Orphaned and left,
Quite forgotten!

THE FLU

Bless you my darling - did you sneeze?
You really must have the flu!
Go to bed, wrap up well,
There's nothing that I can do.

They say feed a cold and starve a fever,
Or is it the other way round?
Here's some tissues, now get some sleep.
I'll catch it too, I'll be bound.

Don't shout of me, I'm not a nurse,
Just beware of the Witches Curse.
Trust you to get the flu!

DENIAL

She never told a soul you know,
She thought it would go away.
But as the days turned into months
It was obviously going to stay.

Her mind was in turmoil,
No solution could she find.
So she simply put it out of her head
And on the matter became quite blind.

The months went by and gathered pace,
Accelerating far too fast.
Each day seemed short, each week just flew.
It was too late now to change the past.

Sooner or later the truth will come out
She thought, almost with relief.
Little did she know the outcome
Would cause a lifetime of grief!

∂

THE THERAPIST

Sometimes in life we meet someone,
Who turns our world around,
By giving us back our self respect
And scraping us off the ground.

Sometimes in life we meet someone
Who is really on our side.
And makes us feel complete again,
By giving us back our pride.

Sometimes in life we meet someone,
When our fortunes are running low.
And I'm glad when it was happening to me,
That you I got to know.

❧

NO ESCAPE

Aren't we all just products,
Of what has gone before?
Although we think we've left the past,
We never quite shut the door!

❧

CAKE AND EAT IT

I'm investing in you,
To make sure that you're true.
But will you forgive,
My indiscretion or two?

THE GOSSIP

She had to be the first to know
And spread the gossip around.
She loved to tickle-tackle
Though at her, people frowned.
She was the local herald
Of bad tidings far and near.
But what did we know of her business?
Well, nothing – gosh- no fear!

BLACK

Black so sombre,
Black so strong.
Black so solid,
Black belongs.

Black is power,
Black is strength.
Black is smart
At any Length.

Black's a suit,
Black's a tie.
Speak out of turn
And black's an eye.

Black stands out,
Black is loud.
And when it rains,
Black's a cloud.

LIFE'S HIGHWAY

Until I know I cannot say.
No plans have I after today.
I have no ties, I must be free.
Married life is not for me.

I'll still be friends, I'll keep in touch.
Life's highway I love so much.
Life's highway 'tis calling me back,
Life's blood to me, the beaten track.

Forget me now and stop the pain,
Loving me is all in vain.
I may return, sometime, someday,
Passing through on life's highway.

Life's highway and paths unknown
To me will always be my home.

OLD VILLAGER

Hiya, Sweetie, thanks for the note,
As usual, hand delivered!
You took the time to go outside,
When most of England shivered.

I got to thinking, that it's been some time
Since my poetic mind awoke!
We've been running hither and thither,
And inundated with folk.

Now that can be a blessing,
As I'm sure you know that's true!
But in this crazy, madcap world,
There's no time for what we *want* to do!

Everyone's so heavily committed,
To trying to make a buck.
But after working flat out,
The rest is down to luck.

So at times when we go missing,
Or retreat to staying in bed.
It's simply because we're knackered,
That word just popped into my head!

The luncheon was quite splendid,
And the ladies found you charming.
But when one asked you if you drove,
I did find *that* alarming!

Was she looking for a set of wheels,
To ferry her about?
She doesn't know you're 90,
Of that, I have no doubt.

The speaker was very human
And in good 'nick' for his age.
His wife is nineteen years younger,
But to go into *that* – I'd need another page!

～

MOODS

The dark side of my sanity
Somehow keeps me sane,
Though black moods I encounter
Are full of untold pain.

But sleep is restful, sleep is bliss,
Sleep will put an end to this.

With the new sun comes the changes
Alters life and rearranges.

Depression gone, I now move on
To a new day, rich with joy.

Sometimes up, sometimes down,
It's part of being human.

The leaves of summer have now turned brown,
Life is but a circle.

❧

PAYBACK TIME

If you believe in Karma,
Then practice it, before it's too late.
Or else 'payback time' will finish you off,
Without any help from Fate!

A WILL TO LIVE

Hang on in there, hold on tight.
Don't slip into tomorrow, tonight.

I must ask some questions before you go,
There's something I really have to know.

Where's the treasure, where's the gold?
You promised to tell me, when you were old.

Don't drift off yet, not until,
You've told me for certain that I'm in your will.

It's no use leaving it to brother Jack,
He's in the next ward with a heart attack.

Don't go yet, I love you dearly.
Is it in the attic – tell me really?

What do you mean, you're feeling better!
Why are you tearing up that letter?

How are you walking away from your bed,
I thought in a minute, that you'd be dead!

THE SELFISH ONE

Forever faithful,
Forever true.
I can't speak for myself
But I expect it of you!

TURMOIL

When emotions are running high,
And logic has gone out of the window.
When all sense of hope is gone
And life is but a faint glow.

When all we can do is take stock
And somehow try to get through.
We can still manage a smile
And even a joke or two!

Try to keep each day normal,
Said some very meaningful friend.
Try to just love each other,
Until life's sweet, bitter end.

When emotions are still running high
And each day sees a new destination,
With yet another hill to climb
All that's left is determination.

Then finally, acceptance sets in,
And we're in the cul-de-sac of 'No Hope'.
We wander in utter disbelief
No more straws are there left to grope.

It's now that we feel reflective,
And relive in our minds the good times.
As we gaze up at the old church clock,
As on the hour, he once again chimes.

That was it then, that was OUR book.
And what a good read it made.
For one thing I'm ever grateful,
We never lived life in the shade.

PHONING GRANDMA

She's gone to Curlybobs for a blow up
Grandad said when I rang today.
So I said that I'd call her back later,
Well, really – what more could I say?

❧

DAISY CHAIN

What's the sense in reacting
To a situation you cannot change?
Try to put it behind you
For in worrying, no hope will you gain.

It's something that cannot be solved
And it's here that you've got to remain.
So what's the sense in reacting?
Life is simply a daisy chain.

NEW START

So you're off tomorrow, I can't stop you now,
There's nothing for you here, I don't blame you somehow.
I know you begged me to come along,
I've given it some thought, but I'm not that strong.

I wish you luck,
Keep in touch,
I'll miss you very much.

I can't come to the airport, It'll upset me I know.
I'll pop round in the morning to say, 'Cheerio'.
As soon as you land, drop me a letter.
I hope that your life turns out to be better.

I wish you luck,
Keep in touch.
I'll miss you very much.

When you have settled, if you still feel the same
And through all the sun you can still see rain.
Well, maybe we'll both have to think again,
But I'll remain here alone, until then.

I wish you luck,
Keep in touch,
I'll miss you very much.

ECSTASY

Oriental gentleness,
A touch beyond compare.
A trip right into fantasy,
To a place no longer there.

Naked, daring.
A tour of delight.
A secret visit,
To a splendid site.

A cultural passage,
With satin walls.
Where velvet carpets line
Magnificent halls.

Ostrich feathers,
Old fashioned lace.
That silky feeling
Around your face.

Come to me,
I'll make you whole.
My uplifted body
Will soothe your soul.

REUNITED

Thank God, we are all back together,
Under her breath, she did utter to me.
But she knew in her heart of hearts,
A solution this could never be.

UNTIMELY DEATH

So suddenly the changes come!
Without warning or any insight.
We got up this morning as a couple,
But I'll be alone in bed tonight.

It's a total shock to the system.
All meaning disappears from life.
This evening I am a widow,
But this morning I was a wife.

This situation is nonsensical.
It beggars belief, yet it's true.
How can I live a minute longer.
Now that I don't have you?

You were the centre of my universe,
My stability, my solid rock.
This feeling of grief is unbearable.
I haven't had time to take stock.

So suddenly the changes arrive,
And upset the master plan.
God give me the strength to carry on,
Now that I've lost my man.

AIR TRAVELLERS

The geese are going to warmer places,
Sensing it's time to go.
They don't require tickets and cases,
They travel lightly – you know.

CASTRATION

He's had his 'diddly dums' cut off,
Like all good tom cats should.
If I could book by husband in,
For sure, you know I would!

TRAPPED

Oh, what fun it is,
Chasing the chaste!
But once in her web
I retreat – post haste.

ONLY SON

He'd been a loner for most of his life,
No one ever knew what he did.
He'd ruled the roost at home as well,
He was always a 'latch key' kid.

His parents came home shocked one night,
A note said he'd gone to Madrid.
He sure had the confidence of an only child,
When he staged his first freedom bid.

THE BIG QUESTION

Should we have children?
She asked her aunts
As they all sat together one day
In the house where there'd
Been a near tragedy.
One aunt said, 'Well love,
'Look at it this way.

'If you've none to make you laugh,
'None will make you cry.'
(Both these aunts were childless,
I have to say).
Then the other one said,
'Ee, I wouldn't bother,
'Look at what's happened here today.'

THE PASSING

Light at the end of the tunnel at last,
It's been a dark passage but now it's past.

Death of a close loved one, that we have known,
Is a pain that we have to endure on our own.

No words of comfort can help us through,
Take a day at a time is all we can do.

We have to believe that they're not far away,
And that united again, we will be some day.

FOOLED

He led her up the garden path,
And offered her his hand,
But his fingers were so slippery,
Life was anything but grand!

LATE NIGHT PASS

It's back to Cold Comfort Farm tonight.
My outing with the chaps is all done.
I'm not sure what awaits my return,
She might even be armed with a gun!

FREE SPIRIT

She always was quite different,
Her mind was so untamed.
From the womb she came screaming, 'Freedom'
Or, so her Mother claimed!

She always was so carefree,
Nothing really fazed her, ever.
She always had the solution,
In fact she was very clever.

She was on another planet,
To her normal fellow man.
She loved her moments of solitude,
Which not many say they can.

You could never tie her down,
Her heart it was on loan.
She was generous to a fault,
But her time, it was her own.

I don't know where she is now.
One day she just blew away.
But I'm better off for knowing her,
She makes me smile on a gloomy day.

☙

UNREST

Wheelie bins marching to the bottom of the drive,
Waiting for the dustcart to arrive.
Millions of nappies in landfill sites,
The idle unemployed shouting their rights.

Worldwide litter louts happily kick the can
Causing distress to their fellow man.
He broke the law and was made to pay,
Now sleeping rough in a shop doorway.

Reduced to begging out on the street,
No sign of policemen out on the beat.
Mindless joyriders stealing cars,
For God's sake, get them put behind bars.

What a drug sodden place this has become!
It wouldn't have done for my gran or my mum.
It's a sorry world and the bad are winning,
Where are the people we used to see grinning?

There's something coming – mankind is scared.
I dare not utter another word.

SELF INDULGENCE

Look where not caring has got us.
Our selfishness has come of age.
It's every man for himself these days,
People are so full of rage.

TSUNAMI

The timing wasn't right,
But then – is it ever?
So many plans on hold
Until the twelfth of never.

Schemes and dreams all squashed,
Swept out to sea so fast.
What they had got lined up
Like history, now is past.

Tidal waves still flood the mind,
The horror, daily comes to visit.
The hopelessness of those poor souls,
To just have fun was their requisite.

The ones who came by chance
Looked fate into its eye.
Whilst others booked their journey,
Well before the tide was high.

Disastrous though it was,
Gladly some lives were saved.
Such lucky ones indeed.
For whom destiny's path was paved.

Alas, it's thought provoking
And it proves the sea is cruel.
This greater force around us
Is such a powerful tool.

BIDING TIME

He knew she'd been seeing his best friend
And it cut him to the core.
If he couldn't trust the people closest to him,
Whatever was he living for?

He decided to try and ignore it
And left them to carry on
Thinking they were fooling him,
Though his faith in humanity had gone.

Behaving the same towards both of them
Seemed to help him cope with the pain.
Why should he upset the status quo,
When he'd so little left to gain.

Eventually the fling just fizzled out.
Instinct told him it had run it's course.
Then, with a self satisfied smile on his face,
He hit her with papers for divorce!

OVERLOOKED

'Hi Dad, it's me, is Mum there?'
She said as he picked up the phone.
That his daughter never chatted with him,
Made him feel so very alone.

STEPPINGFORTH

Thinking, planning, hoping scheming.
Wondering what's the point of dreaming.

Longing, feeling, wanting more.
Touching on what's gone before.

Stumbling, falling, deeper still.
Losing is a bitter pill.

Looking forward, now at last.
Close the chapter on the past.

RECOVERY

You're not alone, so don't feel isolated,
It happens, it's life.
We are all just as vulnerable.

You just have to deal with it,
Move forward, move on.
We are all at times gullible.

We've all been to hell and back.
It's hollow, it's dark.
But the crash is recoverable.

OUR DAD

I think I am going crazy,
My Dad died a year ago.
You'd think that I'd be alright by now,
But I'm afraid that just isn't so.

I still miss him, oh, so desperately.
He was a Dad in a million to us.
He went about life in his own quiet way.
Without ever making too much of a fuss.

Our family have all been supportive.
Though at times I know they feel the strain.
Of watching my sister and I suffer,
As we watch our Mother in pain.

This feeling of loss is overwhelming,
Though, people say it gets easier with time.
My friend says to put it in a 'compartment'
And label it 'Father of Mine'.

That way I can start to rebuild my life
And return to my loved ones still here,
Who've stood by me and waited patiently,
To see me smile again, with good cheer.

Life must go on, I know Dad would agree.
And for his sake, I really must try.
To pick myself up and enjoy the rest of my life
Until the time when it's my turn to die.

No other Dad anywhere in the world
Could ever hold a candle to mine.
With the love that he gave and the love that he left,
From now on – I know I'll be fine.

OVER T'HILL

We ear yer goin' overt'hill,
A wek on Sunday, ay but still,
We ope fer yer sake yer don't see rain,
And that young Jack, he don't complain!
Ow did 'is holiday in Portugal go?
Ow was flyin' – did he let yer know?
Our sen, we plan to go to 429
Next Sunday coming, if its fine…
We'll squeeze it in, our diary is full,
Yer know fer uzz life's owt but dull!
More's the pity, more's the pain,
That on the toilet we both now strain!
We've matchin' piles, now ain't that cute?
Well it is 'til the pain gets quite acute.
Ear, I must tell thee before a forgeet,
I've joined a poets society, yeh, that's reet!
You don't 'av t'live in t'neighbourhood.
You've just got t'send in poems reet good.
Thi like 'em best wi' a Lancashire theme.
Praps overt'hill is a bit extreme!
Tha could bi sin as t'enemy yer know.
Tha might av a bit of a Pennines glow!
Yer cannot foo these Lancashire men,
Yer sin as a traitor – der yer ken?
Yer might av bin born whert red rose grows
But tha lives whert white rose surrendered tha knows!

FALL

We are the leaves of autumn,
Falling from the trees.
We clung tightly to the branches,
But we couldn't beat the breeze.

SECURITY

Innovation, integration.
Make the changes,
Update the system.
International interchanges
Help reduce the high inflation.
Economical expectation,
Investigation, interrogation.
We must at all times,
Guard our nation.

❧

CLIMAX

Sweating, panting – the hour is nigh.
Never before have I felt so high.
Intoxicated by love we cry,
As our bodies separate with a sigh.

SEASONS

Dusk is on its way again,
The wintry nights draw in.
Guy Fawkes is around the corner,
Followed closely by snowmen.

Christmas Bells will shortly ring
The season of goodwill.
And then the New Year will be here,
Time never did stand still.

Going forward, month by month.
On and on we go.
Spring will soon be upon us
And March winds will surely blow.

Summer isn't guaranteed
In Britain anymore.
The black clouds overhead tell us
That soon the rain will pour.

OBSESSED

His presence when he enters the room,
His voice so powerful and deep.
He's taken over my heart and mind
Is it any wonder that I can't sleep?

BAD HAIR DAY

Please don't be annoyed with me
But I have a little confession!
I know full well that hairdressing
Is not really my profession.

It happened last night, quite suddenly,
As I dried my mum-in-law's hair.
A pair of scissors jumped into my hands
And caught me quite unaware.

I know that you control her hair.
So I just snipped the bottom ends.
I hope this doesn't wreck your plans
When round your rollers, it next bends!

I made my own hairdryer hood
With a Tesco bag from the shop.
But it got so hot Mother screamed out
'Hell fire, you'd just better stop!'

Hair can be a problem,
Hair can be a pain.
Especially when idiots snip at it
To make your job in vain.

I hope that you'll forgive me
We were all a little bit stressed!
But when we ladies have our hair washed
It stops us feeling depressed!

DISASTER

A family disaster affected her mind,
And sent her somewhat insane.
She ceased to hang on to reality,
Normality never to regain.

WASHDAY

The washer jammed shut today
With all the best bedding inside.
The joy of modern technology,
Oh, how I could have cried.

Our guests were only hours away,
They'd stopped off to pay tribute to 'Di'.
So I had to get my old skates on,
To make sure the bedding was dry!

The engineer said, 'It must be a power cut
That's messed up the system, Madam.
There's a fifty quid call out charge please',
And as I passed him the cheque I said, 'Damn!'

It wouldn't have happened in the 'old days',
Sometimes with progress we must pay the price.
Though a washer completing its cycle
Shouldn't just be the luck of the dice!

I remember when Mondays were washdays,
Come rain, or hail or fog.
And for dinner it was chips and cold meat
And on the fire there'd be a nice log.

Clothes then got pushed through the mangle,
Leaving feminine hands so sore.
I can still now picture that peg bag
As it hung on the back of the door.

Mum scrubbed the flannels for the cricket club,
Which were covered in grass stains so green.
If it rained they were hung from the ceiling
On a clothes rack that's now rarely seen.

Washday was really back-breaking.
And oh, how their arms did ache.
But then, when the ironing was over,
They'd think nothing of baking a cake!

When women got the vote they decided
That clothes they would no longer scrub.
Life was about to get better,
With the invention of the twin-tub!

❧

FRAILTY

Human frailty, damaged minds,
Where loose heart strings sever.
In the end, there's just one place,
Called the twelfth of never.

STRETCHING THE TRUTH

What a total pack of lies you tell,
You oversell your story.
Why not tell it like it is?
Why surround yourself with glory?

DRUNKENESS

Drinking, drinking,
Always thinking
That today I'll stop.

Drinking, drinking,
Always thinking,
That I'm OK, when I'm not.

Drinking, thinking,
My clothes are stinking.
And now I've developed a stutter.

Drinking, blinking,
Always winking,
I'm not far out of the gutter.

Drinking, drinking,
Always thinking,
That death is not far away.

Drinking, thinking,
Into a coma I'm sinking.
Death might come today.

EGOTISM

Breathe the air of self-importance,
Swallow your own success,
Fall in love with your mirror image,
But don't stick around for the mess.

BYGONE DAYS

Victorian values,
Material wealth.
Where are the teachers
From bygone days?

Servants and kings,
Jesters who sing.
Horses and carriages,
Arranged marriages.

Change for the better,
Change for the worse.
But still beware
Of the witches curse.

Edwardian England,
Occupied France.
Please take your partner,
For the next dance.

TEMPTATION

The path of temptation that he once trod,
Led him out of the garden gate.
And into the arms of his lover,
Oh, what a terrible mistake!

He should have been content with what he had,
But he was young and he wanted it all.
Thank goodness he saw the error of his ways,
And was never again tempted to fall.

CHANCE

Plucking at straws,
Grabbing at chances,
Trusting to life's good luck.

Snatching the air,
Never giving a care,
Be careful not to come unstuck.

PREDATORS

Predators strike when we are vulnerable
And at our lowest ebb.
So beware of false companionship
And don't enter into their web.

COMPARTMENTS

Try to keep things in perspective,
Don't go over the well trodden ground.
To keep reliving the past, as was then,
Is destructive, so turn things around.

Try to keep life in compartments,
By keeping a mental file.
That is easily tucked away in a place,
Somewhere in the memory's mile.

Try to keep going forward,
Yesterday is dead and buried.
Look forward to all your tomorrows,
But don't let your today's be hurried.

Try to keep looking cheerful,
While inside you are falling apart.
That way you will trick your brain,
And love will flow to your heart.

࿇

CLEANSING

Wash away my cobwebs
Let our love unfold.
Take me to Utopia,
Before I get too old.

CRICKET 2005

The pace of cricket is changing.
Five day Tests are rare, unless there's been rain.
Which is always the case at Old Trafford,
And hanging around can be such a pain.

The Twenty, Twenty game has brought excitement
And with it a new army platoon,
Who along with the 'Mexican Wave' mob,
Keep us entertained in the afternoon.

When Sobers scored six sixes in an over,
It was thought a 'one off' and something quite rare.
And when Boyks took root at the wicket
The crowd, at times, dozed off in despair.

Botham's era started the revival,
Along with Thommo and Lille, so fast,
And let's not forget the best 'Windies' side ever,
When Marshall and Holding bowled with a blast.

Cricket is no longer an 'old man's sport,
Or just for 'anoraks' clutching the Wisden Book.
It now attracts a much younger audience
And the odd streaker, just can't be mistook.

W.G. Grace would have turned in his grave
And John Arlott would have been lost for words.
Whilst Brian Johnson would have talked about pigeons,
He much preferred to watch those kind of birds!

But whether it's a googly or a Yorker,
Or a 'full toss' caught at silly mid on.
It just wouldn't be summer without cricket
And the 'Ashes' Tests are second to none.

This game of cricket will outlive us all,
Each generation has its favourite side.
So let's get behind this current team
And help them restore some much needed pride.

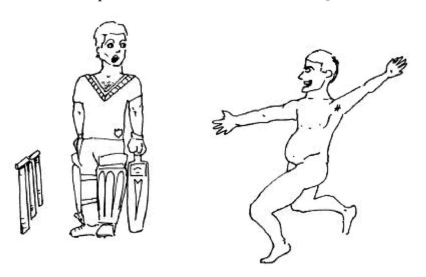

A YES MAN

It cost him his life saying. 'Yes, Dear',
He was constantly over-ruled.
Just staying quiet for peace's sake
Didn't have anyone fooled.

THE VISIT

That powerful, all consuming urge,
When nothing else really matters.
As you block out all the grief in your life,
And in your head the window shatters.

That feeling is beyond compare
And even though you shouldn't be there.
You keep returning again and again,
Into her private lair.

IF ONLY

We all have 'if only' moments
Which stop us from sinking beneath
This game plan of 'rat race' living,
So we survive by the skin of our teeth.

We all have 'if only' thoughts,
Impossible yearnings, so out of reach
From reality as it is, all around us.
If only 'acceptance' they could teach.

SHOCK

All sense of reason has left me today,
I've just found out that my friend is dying.
And all the clichés – so helpfully meant,
Can't prevent this unexpected crying.

ITS TOUGH AT THE TOP

I've had a hard day at the office, dear.
A client took me out for lunch
Then on to his golf club for drinks until four.
I really should have rung you before.

I'm now in a bar full of business contacts.
It pays to be in the right places.
I'll have to go now, my battery's run out.
I shouldn't be late, I'll be home around about.....

I've borrowed a phone from a doll at the bar,
I think that I'd better not drive back by car.
So it might be late when I arrive home,
Did I tell you, that tomorrow, I fly off to Rome?

❧

A FULL LIFE

It's true, we're living longer,
It's great to be so old!
We spend three months abroad
To avoid the winter cold.

We've been taking pills for years now,
It's a wonder we don't rattle.
This getting old, it is no joke,
In fact, it's quite a battle.

We sometimes take a cruise,
Upon the calming seas.
We dine on lavish food,
You can forget the chips and peas!

We go out bowling twice a week
And we also love playing golf.
And then we're off to the cricket
No sitting at home watching Rolf!

We're still so very active
And live life to the full.
What's the point of living in the shade
That would be very dull.

We treasure time together,
Now our salad days have gone.
We just keep making the memories
We'll someday depend upon.

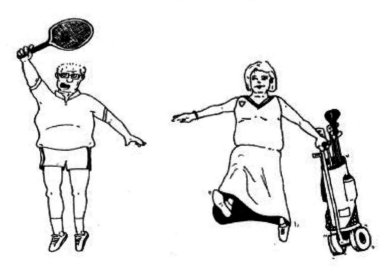